Fighting Words

Tana Reiff

A Pacemaker® *WorkTales* Book

FEARON/JANUS
Belmont, California

Simon & Schuster Supplementary Education Group

WorkTales

Cover illustration: Margaret Sanfilippo
Interior illustration: James Balkovek

Copyright © 1992 by Fearon/Janus, 500 Harbor
Boulevard, Belmont, California 94002. All rights
reserved. No part of this book may be reproduced by
any means, transmitted, or translated into a machine
language without written permission from the
publisher.

ISBN 0-8224-7158-2
Library of Congress Catalog Card Number: 91-70777
Printed in the United States of America
1. 9 8 7 6 5 4 3 2 1

CONTENTS

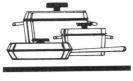

CHAPTER 1

Mamie looked
out the big front window
of the Circle Restaurant.
She watched
a brown-skinned woman
getting off the bus.
So this is
the new waitress,
she said to herself.
"You hired *her*?"
she called back
to Leon, the manager.
She did not sound glad.
"Did you have to pick
a wetback
for me to waitress with?"

"She's a U.S. citizen,"
said Leon.
"What's the problem?"

"No problem at all,"
said Mamie,
not meaning it.
"I only work here."

The new waitress
came in the door.
Leon walked up
to say hello.
"Carmen, this is Mamie.
Mamie, this is Carmen.
You two will be
day waitresses together."

Mamie said "Hi."
But she said it so low
that Carmen didn't hear her.
Carmen put out her hand.
Mamie did not shake it.

"Well, Carmen,
let's get to work,"
said Leon.
"You've worked
in restaurants before.

So I'll just show you
where to find everything.
You'll be working
tables one to six today."

"She gets tables?"
Mamie asked.
"When I first came here,
I had to start
at the counter."

"You told me
you needed help
with the tables,"
said Leon.
"That's why
I hired a new waitress."

He showed Carmen
the kitchen.
He explained
how things worked
at the Circle.
Just as Carmen
put on her apron,

the lunch crowd
started coming in.

Carmen walked up
to table two
to take an order.
"I'll have
a chicken sandwich,"
said the first man.

"I'll have
a fish sandwich,"
said the second man.

"That's a *cheek-in*
and a *feesh*,"
Carmen said back.

The two men
began to laugh.
"That's right,"
joked the first man.
"A *cheek-in*
and a *feesh*!"

Mamie heard
what was going on.
She, too, began to laugh.
"Can't you speak English?"
she said to Carmen.
"If you can't speak English,
you shouldn't work here!"

Carmen looked down.
"My first language
is Spanish,"
she said.
"I speak English
the best I can."
She went to the kitchen
to put in the order.
Then she waited
on another table.

A few minutes later,
Mamie went
to put in an order.
"Chicken and fish are up!"
the cook called out.

"Hear that?"
Mamie called to Carmen.
"Your *cheek-in* and *feesh*
are up!"

"You can stop right now,"
said Carmen.
"I'm going to say
a lot of things
that won't sound right to you.
I'm sorry if you don't like it.
That's the way I talk."

"You can talk
any way you like,"
said Mamie.
"But I say,
if you can't speak English,
go back to your own country!"

"This *is* my country,"
said Carmen.
"I'm staying
right where I am."

Thinking It Over

1. Do you believe
   that everyone
   in the same country
   should speak
   the same language?
   Why or why not?

2. Do you ever judge someone
   before you know them?
   How can this cause trouble
   between people?

3. Do you think employees
   should have a say
   in hiring new people?
   Why or why not?

CHAPTER 2

Business was slow
during the late afternoon.
That was the time
Mamie liked to chat
with the people.
One day,
she was talking
with two older women.

"I just don't like
people with brown skin,"
Mamie told them.
"Now, I'm black,
so I have nothing
against black people.
And I've waited on white people
my whole life.
I have nothing
against white people.
But I don't like

these people with brown skin.
They're not white or black.
I don't know what they are.
Their skin
is the color of dirt.
They look dirty all the time!
And they smell
like rice and beans!"

Mamie didn't know
that Carmen could hear her.
She found out
back in the kitchen.

"Why do you say
I am dirty?"
Carmen asked Mamie.

"I didn't say
you were dirty,"
said Mamie.

"Well, I think
you are lazy,"
said Carmen.

"You're lazy
just like all black people.
You're out there talking
like there's no work to do.
I'm back here
cleaning the kitchen.
This place is a mess!
If the board of health
ever comes in,
they would shut us down!"

"I am not lazy,"
said Mamie.
"I've been working here
for ten years.
I talk with the people
every afternoon.
Leon doesn't mind.
So don't call me lazy!"

"Fine, I won't,"
said Carmen.
"I'll just stop
cleaning the kitchen
and go talk, too!"

Mamie walked by
as Carmen was talking
to a family of four.
"If you want good service,
you sit at my tables,"
she heard Carmen saying.
"That Mamie is so lazy.
You don't want her.
And did you know,
she isn't married
to her old man?
But she lives with him.
Isn't that just like
black people?"

Mamie went
to tell Leon
what she had heard.

"I want
the two of you
in my office right now,"
he said.
"I want
to talk with you both."

Thinking It Over

1. Do you believe
   that all people
   of a certain color or group
   are the same?

2. Why do some people
   put down other people?

3. Why is it important
   to try to get along
   with others on the job?

CHAPTER 3

"Now listen up!"
Leon told Mamie and Carmen.
"We are running
a restaurant here.
People come to the Circle
for a good meal.
They don't come
to hear two women
fighting all the time.
I want you both
to stop it.
What's more,
I want you
to get along like friends.
Or at least
like good co-workers!
Do you understand?"

They both said they did.
They both went back out.

They got along
the rest of the afternoon
by not talking
to each other.

But the next day,
trouble started again.
The family of four
came in again.
This time, they sat
at one of Mamie's tables.
Carmen spotted them
out of the corner
of her eye.
Seeing the family
at Mamie's table
made her angry.
This was the family
she had told to sit
at one of *her* tables!
What were they doing
at one of Mamie's?

Just then,
a party of six

came in the door.
They, too, sat
at one of Mamie's tables.
When they sat down,
Mamie was busy
with another table.
So Carmen walked up
to take their order.

She wrote down
everyone's order.
"I'll be back *pronto*!"
she told them.

She headed
for the kitchen.
Mamie was at the door
waiting for her.
"What do you think
you are doing?"
she asked Carmen.
"You stole my table!"

"You were busy,"
said Carmen.

"You know
that stealing tables
is not how things work,"
screamed Mamie.
"You just want
more tips!
You already took away
half my business!"

"Well, you took
that family of four!"
Carmen screamed back.

"I did not!"
said Mamie.
"They sat down
at my table.
You're just being
a wetback!
You people
pay no mind
to rules.
You make up your own.
And if you don't get
what you want,

you steal it!
Do you think
you are special?"

   "Who are you
to tell me such things?"
Carmen asked.
"I'm telling Leon."

   "Go ahead,"
said Mamie.
"But if you do,
I'll tell Leon
you stole my table."

   "Take your table back!"
Carmen cried.
"It's yours.
Are you happy now?"

Thinking It Over

1. Do you think
   Carmen should have waited
   on the people at Mamie's table?

2. What would you do
   if a co-worker
   was saying mean things
   about you?

3. How do you think
   Mamie and Carmen
   might work out their problems?

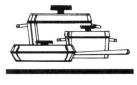

CHAPTER 4

Carmen did not tell Leon
about the things
Mamie had said to her.
But Mamie went to Leon
the next day.

"That woman
is nothing but trouble,"
said Mamie.
"Ever since she came here,
she's been making my life hard.
I can't take it.
It's her or me, Leon.
Take your pick."

"What do you mean—
her or me?"
Leon asked.

"You either fire her
or I will leave,"
said Mamie.

"I don't want you
to leave this place,"
said Leon.
"You've been working here
for ten years.
You're the best waitress
I've got."

"Well, I don't like wetbacks,"
said Mamie.
"And I *really* don't like
that wetback named Carmen."

"I'll tell you again,"
said Leon.
"Carmen is not a wetback.
She is not only legal,
she's a U.S. citizen.
She has
as much right to be here
as you do."

"She can't speak English,"
said Mamie.

"She doesn't speak English
like you do,"
said Leon.
"But she can speak English.
And even if she couldn't,
she's a good waitress."

"Does a good waitress
steal tables
from another waitress?"
Mamie asked.
"Does a good waitress
tell stories
about another waitress?
Answer me that, Leon."

"I'll talk to her,"
said Leon.
"I'll make sure
she stops that stuff.
Now, tell me you will stay
if we can

work things out
with Carmen."

    "I'll give it two weeks,"
said Mamie.
"If Carmen
doesn't change her act
in two weeks,
I'm out of here."

    Mamie went out
to wait on some tables.
After the lunch rush,
Leon called Carmen
into his office.

Thinking It Over

1. Have you ever felt
   that either you or another
   employee
   would have to leave?
   What happened?

2. How might Leon
   help Mamie and Carmen
   work out their problems?

3. How should co-workers
   get along with each other?
   Do they have to be friends
   to work well together?

CHAPTER 5

"Why did you steal
Mamie's table?"
Leon asked Carmen.
"Why did you talk about her
behind her back?"

"Mamie started the trouble,"
Carmen told Leon.
"I just came here
to do a good job.
She decided not to like me
from the start."

"I guess you both
cooked up some trouble,"
said Leon.
"I'll tell you what.
You and Mamie and I
are going to have
a little talk.

All three of us.
I'll help you two
work things out together.
What do you say?"

"I will give it a try,"
said Carmen.

Mamie also said
she would try.

Mamie, Carmen, and Leon
met in Leon's office
the next afternoon.

"First," Leon began,
"we will lay down
some ground rules.
There are five rules.
One, when someone
is talking,
no one else will talk.
Two, no name calling.
Three, what is said here
stays here.

No one else will know
what we talked about.
Four, everyone
will tell the truth.
And, five,
we will try our best
to work out our problems.
Remember that we're here
to work out a problem.
The problem
is not either of you.
The problem
is the problem.
Will you both
go along with these rules?"

    Both women
said they would.

    "Now, each of you
can tell your story,"
Leon went on.
"Just remember the ground rules."

    Mamie explained
that one time
she lived next door
to a family
of Spanish-speaking illegals.
She was always afraid
they would get caught.
She was afraid
she would get into trouble
with the law
because she knew
they were illegals.
She didn't even like
the family.
They cooked foods
she didn't like to smell.
The smell of the food
blew into her house.
She couldn't understand them
when they talked.
From that time on,
she didn't like anyone
with brown skin.

"Just a minute,"
said Leon.
"Are you saying
that everyone with brown skin
is the same?"

"No," said Mamie.
But, she explained,
the way Carmen acted
made her think
of that family of illegals.
She didn't like it
when people made up
their own rules.
She felt
that everyone should live
by the same rules.
Everything was fine around here
until Carmen came
and started stealing tables.
And she didn't like it
when Carmen talked
about Mamie's home life.

Then it was Carmen's turn.
She said
that Mamie had it in for her.
She said
she was only trying
to do a good job.
She said
that all black people
were lazy.
She said
Mamie was being lazy
while she worked hard
in the kitchen.
The only reason
she stole Mamie's table
was that she was angry.

"That's not
a good reason!"
Mamie broke in.

"We're not going to talk
when someone else

is talking,"
Leon said.
"Go ahead, Carmen."

"That's all
I have to say,"
said Carmen.

Then Leon went over
what Mamie and Carmen had
    said.
"Mamie, I hear you saying
all Spanish-speaking people
are the same.
You say
they smell the same.
You can't understand
the way they talk.
You say
they all act the same.
You say
they break rules.
Do I hear right?"

"Yes," said Mamie.

   Leon went on.
"Carmen, you seem to think
Mamie is not being fair to you.
That makes you angry.
So you strike back
by stealing her table
and talking about her.
And I hear you saying
that black people are lazy
and that includes Mamie.
Are these the things
you were saying?"

   "Yes," said Carmen.

   "OK," said Leon.
"You know what I think?
I don't think we're talking
about skin color.
I think there's more to it
than that.
Let's talk
about the real reasons
you two don't get along."

Thinking It Over

1. If you were Mamie,
   why would you be angry
   with Carmen?

2. If you were Carmen,
   why would you be angry
   with Mamie?

3. What do you think
   are "the real reasons"
   Mamie and Carmen
   don't get along?

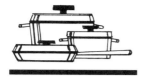

CHAPTER 6

"Mamie," Leon went on.
"I want you to remember
what things were like
before Carmen came.
You were so busy
you didn't know
which end was up.
You begged me
to hire another waitress.
I hired Carmen.
All of a sudden,
you didn't have everyone
all to yourself.
That gave you
less tips."

"I wanted help,"
said Mamie.
"But I'm making
less money now.
That hurts."

"Leon hired me
to do a job,"
said Carmen.
"I wasn't trying
to take money from Mamie."

"I see
another thing,"
Leon went on.
"You two women
do some things
in different ways.
Mamie likes to talk
to the people
during the afternoon.
Carmen would rather
clean up the kitchen.
How does that
make you feel, Mamie?"

"She makes me
look lazy,"
said Mamie.
"But I don't like it
when she *calls* me lazy."

"How about you?"
Leon asked Carmen.

"Sometimes I know
I am doing more work,"
said Carmen.

"See, I believe
you two got off
on the wrong foot,"
said Leon.
"But I believe
there are things
that you both want
from this job.
You may be
more alike than different.
Let's think of things
that you both want."

Mamie and Carmen
looked at each other.
They both
came up with ideas.
They made a list.

1. We both want
   to be good waitresses.
2. We both want
   to run a good restaurant.
3. We both want people
   to enjoy eating
   at the Circle.
4. We both want
   to give good service.
5. We both want
   to make good tips.
6. We both want
   to get along.

"The two of you
want many of the same things,"
said Leon.
"Now how can you get
what you both want?"

Thinking It Over

1. Think of someone
   you are having trouble with.
   What might be
   the real reasons
   you don't get along?

2. What things
   do you both want?

3. What could you do
   that would make
   both of you happy?

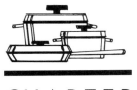

CHAPTER 7

The next day,
Mamie, Carmen, and Leon
met again.
They wanted
to find ways to get
what both women wanted.
Carmen and Mamie
sat side by side
at the table.
Leon sat across from them.

"I have an idea!"
Carmen started.
"We could try
being nice to each other."

"You mean like
I don't make fun
of the way you talk,"
said Mamie.

"Right,"
said Carmen.
"And I won't talk
about you and your old man."

"Fine," said Mamie.
"But what should we do
if we get angry
with each other?"
Mamie asked.

"Maybe we
could talk it over,"
Carmen piped up.

"And we
should always be nice
to the people
who eat here,"
said Mamie.

"Give them good service
no matter how we feel
about each other,"
said Carmen.

"What about
stealing tables?"
Mamie asked.
"I say
that no one
should steal tables."

"That's fair,"
said Carmen.
"And we
should not tell people
to sit at our own table."

"What about tips?"
asked Mamie.
"I don't see
how we can both
make good money."

"I could wait on
the counter sometimes,"
said Carmen.
"Like when
someone sits down

at the counter
and not at a table."

   "That sounds good,"
said Mamie.
"I can handle
a few more tables
than I have now."

   "And if one of us
needs help,
the other can help her,"
said Carmen.
"That way,
people will finish up faster
and we can seat
more people."

   "That's a good idea,"
said Mamie.
"I hate
watching people leave
when they have to wait
for a table."

"And one more thing,"
added Carmen.
"We should not
judge each other
by our skin color."

Mamie looked
at Carmen.
She looked her
right in the eye.
It was the first time
Mamie had ever looked Carmen
in the eye.
For the first time,
she saw Carmen
as a person.
She wasn't sure yet
if she liked her.
But she could not hate her
when she saw her
as a person.

Thinking It Over

1. What does it take
    for you to look at a person
    as a real person?

2. What ideas can you think of
    that would help
    you and another person
    get along better?

CHAPTER **8**

Leon started writing
a new list.
On this list
were the rules
that Carmen and Mamie
would always go by.
"These rules
do not come from me,"
said Leon.
"They come
from the ideas
the two of you came up with."

Here is the list
that Leon wrote.

1. We will be nice
   to each other.
2. If we have a problem,
   we will talk it over.

3. We will give good service
   no matter how we feel
   about each other.
4. We will not
   steal tables
   from each other.
5. We will not tell people
   to sit at our own table.
6. Carmen will wait on
   the counter
   when needed.
7. We will
   help each other out
   when needed.
8. We will not
   judge each other
   by our skin color.

   "Can you both
work by these rules?"
Leon asked.

   Carmen watched
Mamie's face.
She caught Mamie's eyes

watching her, too.
"Yes,"
they both said at once.
They shook hands
and got up to leave.

"Just a minute,"
Leon said.
He picked up
the list.
He pinned it up
on the door.
"Don't forget
it's here!"
he laughed.
"You can check this list
any old time."

"Yes, yes,"
Mamie said.
"We had better hurry.
The lunch crowd
is almost here."

  "One more matter,"
said Leon.
"Suppose one of you
breaks a rule.
What will you do
if that happens?"

  "Rule number two,"
said Carmen.
"We will talk it over.
We will work it out
between us.
Don't you worry."

  "OK," Leon said.
"But remember something.
I'm always here
to help out."

Thinking It Over

1. Do you think
   making a list of rules
   is a good idea?
   Why or why not?

2. What does it mean
   when two people shake hands?

3. Why can it help
   to talk over problems?

CHAPTER 9

All the long talks
between Carmen and Mamie
were worth the trouble.
It helped them
treat each other
like people.
Having that list
up on the door
worked wonders.
Both women
knew the rules.
They both
stopped to read them over
every day.

One day Mamie
was reading the list
on the door.
Carmen walked by

as she read.
"Look at that!"
said Carmen.
"Have you ever read
that paper up there
from the board of health?"

    Mamie looked up
at the paper
on the wall.
"No," she said.
"Can't say as I have."

    "Well, you better read it,"
said Carmen.
"You never know
when someone
from the board of health
might show up.
We have to make sure
everything is in order."

    "Is that your business?"
Mamie snapped.
"That's Leon's job."

"It's everyone's job,"
said Carmen.
With that,
she went out
to wait on a table.

Mamie stayed back
to read the paper
from the board of health.
She saw Leon
heading for the back door.
"I'll be back soon,"
he waved to her.
"I'm just going
down to the bank."

"Your order is up!"
the cook called to Mamie.
She picked up the dish
and headed out
to serve it.

Just then,
Carmen rushed back
into the kitchen.

"Wouldn't you know it?"
she cried.
"Leon just left
and a man
from the board of health
just walked in
the front door!"

Thinking It Over

1. What are the rules
    of the place
    in which you live or work?
    Do you know
    all of them?
    Are they fair rules?

2. Why are there people
    to help other people
    stick to the rules?

CHAPTER **10**

"I don't believe this!"
Mamie laughed.
"Let's fix up
a few things
in the kitchen
before he gets back here."

She ran over
and picked up a pack
of paper napkins.
"We can't have these
on the floor!"
she said.
"I just read that
on that paper."

Carmen pulled off
her dirty apron.
She grabbed
a clean one

and tied it on.
Mamie did the same.

Mamie ran around
to all the counters.
She picked up
a cream pie.
She put it
in the refrigerator.

Carmen threw
her dirty wipe rag
back with the aprons.
She grabbed a clean one
and started to wipe
everything in sight.

Mamie grabbed
a cracked dish
from the cook.
"You can't use
that old thing!"
she told him.
She threw the dish
in the can.

Carmen ran back
into the store room.
She cleaned it up
and put things in order.

The man
from the board of health
walked into the kitchen.
"I came to check up,"
he said.

"Check all you want,"
said Mamie.
"We know your rules!"

He looked around.
"Looks good, looks good,"
he said.
"No paper goods or food
stored on the floor.
Clean aprons.
No food
sitting around
that should be hot or cold.

Let me see
that wipe rag.
OK, that's clean enough.
No cracked dishes
being used for cooking.
Let me take a look
at your store room."

   Carmen took him back.
"Everything looks fine,"
the man said
as he looked around.
"You can tell your boss
his restaurant passed.
I'll send him a letter
next week.
Good day, people."

   And he was gone.

   A few minutes later,
Leon got back.
Mamie and Carmen
told him what had happened.

"Things around here
are pretty much in order,"
said Leon.
"But you two
took care of the fine points.
I thank you both!"

Carmen looked at Mamie.
Mamie looked at Carmen.
"You are good
at doing the talking!"
Carmen laughed.

"You sure know
the health rules,"
said Mamie.
"I guess
this place
needs both of us."

"And you and I
need each other,"
said Carmen.
"Neither of us
could have done it alone."

"Leon, you are
one lucky guy,"
said Mamie.
"Carmen and I
saved your neck!
You have here
the two best waitresses
in town."

Leon laughed.
"And the cleanest kitchen, too!
I say
we all won!"

Thinking It Over

1. Think of a time
   when it took
   more than one person
   to get a job done.

2. What kinds of things
   bring people together?

3. Why does everyone
   need to work together?

4. What has to happen
   to make everyone win?